THEN & NOW®

NEWTOWN SQUARE

Opposite: In the early 1900s, an unidentified horseman prepares to ride through Bartram's Covered Bridge on Goshen Road. (Courtesy of Newtown Square Historical Preservation Society.)

THEN & NOW®

NEWTOWN SQUARE

Christopher Driscoll and Janice Elston

For the individuals and organizations who have contributed toward the preservation of Newtown Square's historic resources.

ISBN 978-0-7385-6528-6

Library of Congress Control Number: 2008940083

Published by Arcadia Publishing
Charleston, South Carolina

Printed in the United States of America

Then and Now is a registered trademark and is used under license from Salamander Books Limited

For all general information contact Arcadia Publishing at:
Telephone 843-853-2070
Fax 843-853-0044
E-mail sales@arcadiapublishing.com
For customer service and orders:
Toll-Free 1-888-313-2665

Visit us on the Internet at www.arcadiapublishing.com

On the front cover: Bartram's Covered Bridge, located at the intersection of Goshen and Boot Roads, spans Crum Creek, dividing Delaware and Chester Counties. It was built in 1860 and is the last remaining covered bridge still standing in Delaware County. At one time, there were at least five covered bridges in Newtown Township and well over 30 in Delaware County. (Courtesy of Newtown Square Historical Preservation Society.)

On the back cover: The Newtown Square Hotel (to the far left) sat just west of the Route 3 and 252 intersection. Once the center of activity in Newtown, it was torn down in 1969 to make way for a branch of the Philadelphia National Bank. (Courtesy of Newtown Square Historical Preservation Society.)

Contents

ACKNOWLEDGMENTS

This book could not have been made without the efforts of former Newtown police chief and Newtown Square Historical Preservation Society founder Stan Short. A lifelong resident, he was a walking history of the township and spent his off hours collecting photographs, stories, and memorabilia for the museum and the society that he was so instrumental in founding. The vast majority of historical photographs in this book come from his famous slide collection. Many Newtown residents were first drawn into the society when they attended one of his slide show presentations and heard the old stories of the township told with his brand of salty humor and honesty. As a lifelong policeman in the Newtown Square, he knew all the secrets of the township and wove them into his presentation. He passed away in 2008. Although his voice is stilled, the efforts of his life live on in the museum, the historical society, and the township that he loved. We dedicate this book to his memory.

The authors would also like to recognize others who contributed to the production of this book, including the board of the Newtown Square Historical Preservation Society, Aronimink Golf Club, Melmark Home, Newtown Square Railroad Museum, Delaware County historian Keith Lockhart, and private historic home owners of Newtown Square. Lifelong Newtown resident Clara (Lewis) McVeigh did a significant amount of original research on the historic buildings and early history of the township. Her work was the basis for *Historic Newtown Township*, published in 1984 by the Newtown Square Historical Preservation Society. All historic photographs are from the collections and archives of the Newtown Square Historical Preservation Society unless otherwise noted. All modern photographs were taken by Christopher Driscoll.

Lastly, the authors encourage readers' participation as members of the Newtown Square Historical Preservation Society. A wealth of information can be found on the historical society's Web site.

INTRODUCTION

Newtown Township was settled in 1681 and incorporated as a township in 1684. In 1681, William Penn planned the "first inland town west of Philadelphia" at the intersection of Goshen Road (laid out in 1687) and Newtown Street Road (laid out in 1683). The township was laid out around a center square or "townstead" of approximately one square mile surrounded by farmland. Newtown is the oldest township in Delaware County. Original purchasers of land in the township received one acre in the townstead for every 10 acres of surrounding farmland. Penn had planned New Town while still in England and was able to sell a considerable number of tracts before leaving there. However, many of these people "never lived on the land." The properties changed hands many times, and early growth of the township was slow.

Newtown was organized as the townstead with the majority of early settlers being Welshmen. These Welsh Friends (Quakers) needed a road to facilitate their journey to meeting; the only established road at the time was Newtown Street Road, which ran north and south. As such, in 1687, an east–west road was laid out (Goshen Road) so the Friends could attend either Goshen or Haverford meetings. By 1696, the Friends had become numerous enough to hold their own meeting in Newtown and continued to gather in a private home until the completion of the Newtown Friends Meeting House in 1711. In the 1700s, Newtown was basically a farming community. Blacksmith and wheelwright shops emerged on the main arteries to service horse-and-buggy travelers. Taverns and inns were also opened to accommodate local patrons as well as drovers taking their livestock to the markets in Philadelphia.

During the 1800s, a number of mills sprang up along Crum Creek (the western border) and Darby Creek (in the northeast corner of the township). These included sawmills, paper mills, shingle mills, and a woolen factory. In the Darby Creek area, a number of tenement houses were built as well as a general store to service the needs of the mill workers.

The name Newtown Square was not formerly established until 1828 when a post office of that name was located near the corner of West Chester Pike and Newtown Street Road. In 1860, the population of Newtown Township was 830; the population of Philadelphia was approximately half a million. At this time, the railroad, called the "iron horse," was laying track out of Philadelphia in all directions, with service to Chester, Media, West Chester, and Radnor . . . but not Newtown. As these towns and stops along the way grew and prospered, mills closed and businesses declined in Newtown. By 1890, the population had fallen to 648.

As an agricultural community, stone farmhouses graced the country landscape throughout the 1800s. Additions were made to the early, simple dwellings as families grew and more living space was required. Prosperity due to a growing market also enabled property owners to make additions not only to their own homes but also on the property and in the form of tenements and outbuildings.

In 1859, the Rose Tree Hunt Club was organized south of the township followed by the Lima Hunt Club to the west (1885) and the Radnor Hunt Club at the intersection of

Darby-Paoli and Goshen Roads (1886). With these developments, many country estates were built in the rolling hills of Newtown for "either country gentlemen of Old Quaker blood . . . or rich Philadelphians who loved hunting, owned good horses, and were not afraid to ride them." Major transportation developments for the township did not occur until the mid-1890s when trolley service was opened to Newtown. Before this time, railroad lines were proposed, but due to a series of reorganizations and competition between companies for right-of-way, as of 1892, no track was laid. In 1894, however, mule-drawn service was initiated by the Philadelphia and Delaware County Railroad, with steam dummies used to help out on the hills. Electrification was completed the following year, and the trolley was open from Newtown to Fernwood in 1895. By 1889, the reorganized Philadelphia and West Chester Traction Company completed the track to West Chester.

At the dawn of the 20th century, the automobile began to disperse urban populations over the countryside. Trolleys, along with the new horseless carriage, transformed country farmers into suburban commuters. Farms were sold and the land subdivided. Newtown boomed. Many city dwellers retained their country estates; however, these became hidden amid gridiron developments. Although construction slackened during the Depression, another boom was experienced after World War II. Today some farms and smaller estates remain, but for the most part, the township was developed into a suburban community with old stone homes and structures dotting the landscape to serve as reminders of days gone by.

In 2009, Newtown is a township with a land area of 10.11 square miles and an estimated population between 10,000 and 16,000 individuals. The actual population of Newtown is difficult to calculate because the number from the 2000 census (16,200 people) for the 19073 zip code includes a significant number of homes outside the township, such as Radnor, Edgemont, and Willistown Townships, that use a Newtown Square mailing address.

As of 2009, the last remaining large, open tracts of land in Newtown are under preparation for development. Episcopal Academy moved its campus from Lower Merion to 123 acres in the northern part of the township in 2008. The Ellis Preserve Town Center was approved after more than four years of intense debate to be located on the former grounds of the Ellis School for Girls. The former 450-acre DuPont estate is due to be developed into an extensive high-end residential neighborhood. The Marville of Newtown town center site planned by a developer on the western side of the township has been cleared for many years.

Over the last several decades, Newtown Square has grown into a highly desirable location because of its central location, wide variety of housing available, and low property taxes. Demographically, real estate agents have labeled Newtown part of the new westward-moving main line, although it is not part of the traditional main line railroad towns. Newtown's sense of history contributes and enhances what makes Newtown Square a special place to live, work, and visit.

The majority of photographs in this book will show drastic contrasts of change over the last century, yet some will look strikingly similar. This is not by accident but achieved by those who shared an appreciation for preservation in years past and by those who continue to contribute to the stewardship of preservation, securing a promising future for the next generations to come.

CHAPTER 1

Community Foundations

The original Newtown Square Hotel was built in the early to mid-1700s and was the center of activity in Newtown Square. Located just west of the intersection of West Chester Pike (Route 3) and Newtown Street Road (Route 252), it was originally called the Newtown Square Inn and was demolished in 1903. The redbrick Victorian building that replaced it was demolished in 1969.

The original Newtown Township welcome signs were replaced with the current green signs sometime in the late 1900s. The "No Gunning" sign was not a welcome addition at the time—notice the bullet holes. The hanging welcome signs at either end of West Chester Pike were donated by the Newtown Square Business Association.

This early-1950s photograph shows township officials at the current Newtown Township building location on Bishop Hollow Road—a 10-acre site given to the township by Sun Oil Company. The township's offices were temporarily located on St. Alban's Circle in the early 1950s between the demolition of the old town hall and construction of the new building. The original building constructed at a cost of $70,000 was formally opened on October 19, 1957. It was expanded in the 1990s to include the Newtown Public Library, which was originally located in the Newtown Square Shopping Center.

The old Newtown firehouse was built in 1916. The original firehouse was demolished in the early 1960s to make way for the current one, which rests in the same location in the center of town on North Newtown Street Road, next to what is currently the Wawa market. Fire service in Newtown has remained volunteer based since its establishment in 1916.

The Newtown Square Friends Meeting House was first built in 1711. In 1791, (due to a fire) the meetinghouse was reconstructed and expanded, using part of the original stone walls. This 200th anniversary photograph from 1915 shows that little has changed in the last 100 years. Inside, the meetinghouse has a sliding partition dividing the building into two sides when it was common for men and women to attend meeting separately. Newtown was settled by mostly Welsh Quakers in the late 1600s.

Newtown Public School No. 1, also known as the Wyola School, was built in 1870. The building was once owned by Jean Austin DuPont, who restored the building in 1970, including the original school bell. Located on North Newtown Street Road, the building is owned by the township and leased to Episcopal Academy, with its new campus property bordering the old school grounds.

Newtown Public School No. 2, also known as the Red Brick Schoolhouse, was originally constructed in 1896 due to an influx of additional children to the area at the time. It was used as a school until 1924. It is located at the intersection of South Newtown Street Road and Alpha Drive. This early-1900s photograph shows that it was completely altered while being converted to its current use as office space.

This photograph shows Marple-Newtown High School, which was originally built in 1914. It burned down in 1956 and was replaced with another school building, which today is the Gauntlet Community Center, named for local businessman Bob Gauntlet.

The Newtown Township Elementary Public School on Bishop Hollow Road was constructed in 1924. Alice Grim served as the first principal, and in 1951, the school was renamed in her honor. The building was expanded in 1953 to include a library, additional classrooms, and administrative offices. As the population of Newtown increased, the Culbertson Elementary School was built on Goshen Road in 1959. The last classes were held at the Alice Grimm School in 1982, and the Delaware County Christian School purchased it a year later to use as its elementary school.

St. Albans Episcopal Church was completed in 1951 and is the namesake for the St. Alban's neighborhood of Newtown Square. St. Alban's Church began as a mission of old St. David's Church and once held service in a collapsible wooden structure on Bishop Hollow Road. The five acres of land for the current church site were purchased from Pennsylvania Hospital Farm, encompassing most of West Chester Pike to Goshen Road and Bryn Mawr Avenue to North Newtown Street Road. This photograph was taken before the church building was expanded in 1971.

CHAPTER 2

Old Roadways and West Chester Pike

This is a 1905 photograph of a Philadelphia and West Chester Traction Company open-air trolley car. It was a popular mode of transportation up and down West Chester Pike. The median strip between the east and west lanes of West Chester Pike are where the tracks once laid.

This early-1900s photograph shows Goshen Road heading west when it was still dirt. The view from approximately where Crum Creek Road intersects Goshen Road shows the William Lewis barn complex clearly visible to the right (currently Echo Valley Farm). The Lewis farm encompassed both sides of Goshen Road and at one time totaled about 600 acres, including most of Echo Valley.

This rare and undated photograph is of the Bishop Hollow Road covered bridge over Crum Creek. The bridge was also known as Matlack's Covered Bridge and was most likely removed in the 1930s when the Geist/Springton Reservoir was constructed. This covered bridge had a Burr arch truss design (like Bartram's Covered Bridge). Another covered bridge once crossed Crum Creek nearby on Gradyville Road. (Courtesy of Keith Lockhart.)

This is an east-facing view of the 1981 tercentennial (300th anniversary) parade for Newtown Township on West Chester Pike. The grand parade was held on May 9, 1981, and included some 150 fire engines, antique cars, floats, marching bands, mounted honor guards, and the First City Troop. The largest parade ever held in Newtown was organized by the Tercentennial Commission, which later became the Newtown Square Historical Preservation Society.

West Chester Pike is seen here facing west near the intersections of Valley View and Surrey Drive. The trees planted up and down the median strip in Newtown Square were first planted in the 1970s, an effort led by then township manager Paul West. The view from the 1970s looks virtually the same today.

This early-1900s photograph is of West Chester Pike looking west from approximately the Clover Lane intersection. The original Pennsylvania Hospital Farm is on the right with the main entrance in the middle just beyond the roadside trees. On the left side is the Hanley farm, which today is the Newtown Square Shopping Center.

This 1950s photograph of West Chester Pike facing west from just beyond the Newtown Square Shopping Center light shows one of the trolley's switches, which allowed other trolleys to pass going the opposite direction on a single track. Right in front of the Hanley farmhouse, this particular switch was known as "Hanley's switch."

This 1950s photograph of West Chester Pike facing west from the St. Alban's Avenue intersection shows the Newtown Square Hotel still standing in the distance, and to the right, the same sign for the Greenhill Diner is still used today by Hills' Seafood. Gasoline at the Gulf station was 27¢ a gallon.

Bishop Hollow Road originally ran straight, meeting West Chester Pike just west of Newtown Street Road. The white sign points the direction to the Newtown Edgemont Little League Field.

The historic photograph was taken in the 1960s. Evidence of the original road still remains today; there is a visible gate blocking the old road from West Chester Pike across from Upper Crust Pizza.

This late-1940s photograph of an automobile accident on Clyde Lane was taken from what is today the intersection of Bishop Hollow Road with West Chester Pike. This area was called the Clyde Lane Shopping Center. The Newtown Square Post Office was at one time located on the right side of Clyde Lane. Today the Videon automobile service building on the left still stands but is no longer in use.

The West Chester Pike and Boot Road intersection is seen here looking west in a photograph from about 1930. The Gulf gasoline station on the right was part of the Kirk Chevrolet Agency. At one time, Thomas Kirk's farm included land on both sides of West Chester Pike at this location. Today the house on the right is Mama's Pizza shop, and the Preston mansion sits behind it on Boot Road.

Looking west on West Chester Pike, this view is from the current SAP property. The trolley tracks have been removed, but the eastbound lanes have not yet been completed in this 1950s photograph. Today the building on the left is the location of Hill's Cadillac, and across the way on the right is now Porsche of the Main Line.

This rare photograph facing to the east was taken just west of Boot Road on West Chester Pike around 1960. The white fence is currently part of the SAP America campus, and the first building to the left is the original Kirk Chevrolet Agency. The trolley tracks had been removed, but the road had not yet been widened to two lanes in both directions. Just to the left of the roofline is the Greenland mansion, which was once used by Ellis College and is now where SAP's main building is located.

This 1970s photograph shows the Truscott Farm barns and outbuildings as viewed from Florida Park. The 231-acre farm was also known as Fox Trail Farms, Aliquippa Farm, and the Bar X Dude Ranch. The farm was sold in 1970, and the property has since been owned by a developer with mixed-use plans for the site. The white barn and farmhouse on the top of the hill to the left are still there and located on Phillips Lane off Boot Road.

Another rare and undated photograph shows the West Chester Pike covered bridge, also known as the Castle Rock Covered Bridge. The bridge crosses Crum Creek and divides Newtown and Edgemont Townships. The bridge was most likely demolished around the dawn of the 19th century. The bridge had what was considered an odd arrangement of trusses, with a queen post over a king post design. This view is from the Rafferty Subaru dealership facing Edgemont Township to the west. (Courtesy of Keith Lockhart.)

The end of the Newtown Square branch of the Pennsylvania Railroad was just north of the Winding Way bypass in this 1950 photograph. This view is from Caley Road and North Newtown Street Road. The dip in the lawn is where the freight station once sat before being moved and restored at its Drexel Lodge location on West Chester Pike. The railroad was taken out of service in 1963, and the tracks were taken up in the 1960s. Evidence of the trestle is still noticeable on Bryn Mawr Avenue near Malin Road.

This undated photograph shows the trimming of trees lining Route 252 facing north on the BPG property just north of the Newtown Street Road entrance. The power lines have since been moved behind the trees.

The Route 252 bypass is seen here facing south in the 1950s before Route 252 was widened. The Wyola Schoolhouse sits in the distance and at the time had a significant front lawn. The old schoolhouse is now about 10–15 feet from the road. This section of the township was known as Wyola, which had its own post office at one time.

CHAPTER 3

The Newtown Square Crossroads

The original Newtown Square Inn is being demolished in this 1903 photograph to make way for a newer hotel building on the same site just west of Newtown Street on West Chester Pike. A section of the old hotel was still used while the new one was constructed. (Courtesy of Keith Lockhart.)

The center of Newtown grew up around the intersection of Routes 3 and 252, hence the name Newtown Square. This 1930s photograph, taken from the southeast side of the intersection, shows from left to right the Newtown Square Hotel; Hanley's Store/Newtown Square Post Office; Ewing's Market, the Great Atlantic and Pacific Tea Company (A&P); and an Atlantic gasoline station. Today only the middle building remains.

This 1940s photograph of West Chester Pike just west of the main intersection with Route 252 shows the Newtown Square Hotel sign on the roof of the building. This was the heart of Newtown Square until the early 1950s. The original ACME Market was located where the Mattress Giant now stands. Mackey's Pharmacy was also located here until moving to its current location farther east on West Chester Pike.

This early-1950s photograph shows the old Newtown Square hardware store at the northwest corner of West Chester Pike and Newtown Street Road. Old deed records show that building's existence dated back until at least 1810 when it served as a general store. The building was razed in 1971 to make way for additional parking for the small shopping center between Newtown Street Road and Clyde Lane. Pictured from left to right are Pat Newby, head of the Newtown road crew; Al Saffren, Newtown's chief of police; and an unidentified road crew worker.

Pictured here in the 1950s is the old town hall after the trolley track was removed. Originally constructed in 1868 on the southeast corner of West Chester Pike and Newtown Street Road, the lower floor of the building was a carriage-making shop, and the second floor was a place for town meetings, society meetings, school graduations, and entertainment. The small additions were added later and included a gasoline station and antique store called Scott, Showalter and Rebman. The hall was torn down in 1955 to make room for the widening of West Chester Pike.

The Horace Lewis house was built around 1850 on North Newtown Street Road just north of West Chester Pike next to the firehouse. Once used as a residence, the building was most recently the home of Doran's Surveying Company. The house was reputedly the general store keeper's house at one time.

Mackey's Pharmacy, Tim's Inn, and the Rodenboh and Baker Real Estate office are seen here in the early 1950s in the shops on the St. Alban's side of West Chester Pike. These buildings were constructed individually rather than as one shopping strip. The exterior of Mackey's Pharmacy is essentially the same as was nearly 60 years ago.

This photograph of St. Alban's Circle was taken in 1967. At the time, Three Country Boys occupied the entire building that Luigi and Giovanni's and Sherwin-Williams currently share. The evergreen tree in the center has grown quite a bit since then and is lit for the holiday season every year by the Newtown Square Fire Company.

Three Country Boys was once located in this two-storefront building on Chapel Road across from the entrance to St. Alban's Church. This photograph from the early 1960s shows that the building has only had minor cosmetic changes in the last 50 years and is now the home of a tailor and a custom clothing store.

Originally built as a large restaurant called the Timbers in the 1970s, this building on West Chester Pike across from the Newtown Square Shopping Center is now shared by Wachovia Bank and Blockbuster Video.

CHAPTER 4

National Register Historic Sites

The Hood Octagonal Schoolhouse is shown here in 1907. The eight-sided, one-room schoolhouse was placed on the National Register of Historic Places in 2006. Built of fieldstone, the design takes advantage of heating, natural lighting, and ventilation of the time. The seven windows are placed high above children's heads purposely to avoid distractions outside the classroom. (Courtesy of Keith Lockhart.)

The Square Tavern, also known as the Square Inn or the John West house, is located at the corner of North Newtown Street and Goshen Road, the original town center of Newtown Township as planned by William Penn. West was once host of the tavern between 1744 and 1758. His son Benjamin West lived on the grounds as a child and went on to become America's first internationally known artist. The Square Tavern was built in 1742 by Francis Elliot; this 1960s photograph shows when it was last used as a residence by families of Ellis College employees.

This late-1970s photograph shows the early beginnings of restoration of the Square Tavern prior to Newtown's 300th anniversary celebration in 1981. The nearly $500,000 restoration by local historic restoration architect John Milner was paid for by Atlantic Richfield Company (ARCO), which at the time owned the grounds of the former Ellis School for Girls. The rear addition was removed at the time of the 1980 restoration.

This 1981 photograph shows the Square Tavern after complete restoration. At one time, the building was used as Delaware County's visitors' bureau headquarters. After years of neglect, the building was again repaired and restored in 2008 by BPG, which owns the tavern and is developing the Ellis Preserve/town center site. The Square Tavern today looks the same as it did after the 1981 restoration. The interior contains five fireplaces, including a walk-in cooking one. The building is made available to tour by the Newtown Square Historical Preservation Society.

The early stages of restoration of the Paper Mill House located at the corner of St. David's and Paper Mill Roads can be seen here around 1980. The house is actually several residences built together that housed those who worked the mills along Darby Creek. The oldest section, closest to St. David's Road, was built in 1770. The house, along with four and a half acres, was sold to the township in the late 1970s. The restoration of the building took many years in the early 1970s and was led by volunteers, headed by Stan Short and Jim Crossan.

This photograph from about 1980 shows the Paper Mill House in mid-restoration. The building is now restored and operates as the Paper Mill House Museum of Newtown Township. The section to the left at one time served as a general store and has been rebuilt to represent this. The house contains a gift shop and 19th-century reproduction rooms on the first floor, meeting space in the basement, historic exhibits on the second floor, and archive space in the attic. The building and property is owned by Newtown Township and managed by the Newtown Square Historical Preservation Society.

This early-1980s photograph shows the beginning stages of reconstruction of the general store that once occupied this same space in the Paper Mill House. The Paper Mill House was home to the general store and four residences for mill workers and their families. Each unit had a separate entrance with no interior doorways connecting the units. The rooms were built above one another—basement, first floor, second floor, and attic—all connected by spiral staircases. Corner fireplaces in the residences had flues leading to a shared, central chimney. The restoration of the Paper Mill House was supported by volunteers, donations, and grants.

This photograph of the second floor of the Paper Mill House prior to restoration shows the current historical exhibit space. This particular exhibit was updated in 2008. Plans are under way to update the remaining exhibit areas of the Paper Mill House, as well as other updates and improvements to the interior and exterior of the building.

This early-1960s photograph of Bartram's Covered Bridge shows its extensive state of disrepair at the time. The bridge was first repaired in the late 1960s by the then Marple-Newtown Historical Society. The bridge was restored again more extensively in 1996 and funded by a combination of donations and grants. The bridge is currently maintained by the Bartram Bridge Joint Preservation Commission with members from both Newtown and Willistown Townships. More information is available at the commission's Web site.

This 1930s photograph shows the Bartram's Covered Bridge from the Willistown side facing east at a time when the bridge was still in active use. Located at the intersection of Goshen and Boot Roads, the bridge was built in 1860 by Ferdinand Wood, who designed the portals to be "Hi and Wide as a Load of Hay." The bridge is 80 feet long by 13 feet wide. The truly unique feature of this covered bridge is the portal sheathing, considered to be the only covered bridge featuring this design. The bridge crosses Crum Creek, the dividing line between Newtown and Willistown Townships. The cost of $1,133 to build the bridge was shared by both Delaware and Chester Counties.

For the supporting arches, Bartram's Covered Bridge uses a Burr truss design, named after Theodore Burr, a Connecticut carpenter who patented the design used in many covered bridges. In this early-1990s photograph, the arch can be seen from the outside connecting to the foundation. The photograph today is from a slightly different downstream angle when the bridge was lit for the holidays in December 2008. The bridge is named for Mordecai Bartram, who was instrumental in its building.

The Hood Octagonal Schoolhouse is shown here in an early-1900s photograph. The eight-sided schoolhouse located on the eastern grounds of Dunwoody Village on West Chester Pike has been used as an iconic symbol for Dunwoody Village, the township, and the Marple-Newtown High School. Once believed to have been originally constructed in 1798, the schoolhouse was actually built in 1841 and only operated for 25 years before being abandoned. After years of decay, the schoolhouse was restored in 1963 through a bequest of a Dunwoody Home resident. The building is maintained by Dunwoody Village and made available for tours.

This photograph from about 1895 shows old St. David's Church, built in 1715, which is regarded as one of the most beautiful churches in the original 13 colonies. Poet Henry Wadsworth Longfellow penned a poem called "Old St. David's at Radnor" about St. David's Church in 1880. While it actually sits in a far corner of Newtown Township, the location of the old church is often confused, being listed in Radnor, St. David's, and Devon. The newer, larger church on the opposite side of Valley Forge Road is located in Radnor Township. (Courtesy of Keith Lockhart.)

This photograph of old St. David's Church from about 1909 shows that the ivy was removed from the stone walls. In addition, a covered entranceway was added since 1895. All the window and door hardware was replaced in 1893 except for the main door lock. The small interior contains 23 wooden pews and benches, installed in 1830 (replacing the 17 previously existing).

Old St. David's Church is the oldest extant non-Quaker parish in Delaware County. The cornerstone was laid on May 9, 1715, and much of the subsequent building was done by parishioners in the traditional Welsh country church style—simple, rectangular, one-room buildings. (Courtesy of Keith Lockhart.)

This 1970s photograph shows old St. David's Church with Gen. "Mad Anthony" Wayne's grave and monument in the foreground. The monument was erected in 1811 and presumably designed by William Strickland, who designed a similar marker for the Paoli Massacre site nearby. Old St. David's was the home church of Wayne, a famous Revolutionary War officer and Native American fighter. Wayne's mother and grandparents lived in Newtown Square on St. David's Road in the Iddings house. Wayne's mother is buried in the Seventh Day Baptist Cemetery on North Newtown Street Road.

This undated vintage photograph shows Gen. "Mad Anthony" Wayne's grave facing from old St. David's Church. Wayne died on December 15, 1796, in battle at Fort Presque Isle on Lake Erie. He was buried at that location, but in 1809, his son Col. Isaac Wayne exhumed the body, boiled the bones, and brought them back to Newtown on horseback to be buried at St. David's churchyard. Legend has it that on the long and bumpy final journey from one corner of the state to the other, the trunk kept falling off and breaking open, losing bones along the way, and that Isaac was in such as rush that he did not notice bones falling out until he reached home. So now on each New Year's Day, Gen. "Mad Anthony" Wayne's birthday, his ghost rises from the grave at old St. David's Church and rides across the state searching for his missing bones.

CHAPTER 5

Private Historic Homes

The three-story Georgian DuPont mansion seen here in the 1970s was built in 1925 as an exact replica of James Madison's Virginia estate, Montpelier. The DuPont estate has been called Liseter Hall Farms and Foxcatcher Farms over the years. In the 1920s and 1930s, the farm was considered to have the best horse facilities in the mid-Atlantic, producing outstanding racehorses. The mansion is still visible along the west end of the Goshen Trail and is slated to be demolished when the estate is developed into a high-end residential community.

Known as the Hood Fawkes house, the childhood home of William Dunwoody was built around 1770. His mother's family, the Hoods, lived here for many generations. Dunwoody made his fortune in Gold Medal Flour (later General Mills) in Minneapolis. A philanthropist, his will stated that the old homestead should be operated as a farm and home for convalescent men, which today is Dunwoody Village. The house, shown here in the 1970s, is not in use and is located beyond the octagonal schoolhouse and the Dunwoody barn complex.

This 1970s photograph shows the north side of the John Hunter house on College Avenue. The home was built in 1722 when John Hunter came to Newtown along with Gen. "Mad Anthony" Wayne's grandfather. The Hunters were among the earliest settlers in Newtown Township.

The Fox Chase Inn on West Chester Pike was first built in 1724. Between 1781 and 1813, the tavern was known as Fawkes Tavern. Because of its location between Philadelphia and West Chester, the inn was a popular wayside stop in 19th-century Newtown. The inn was closed in 1825 and rebuilt before again operating as a tavern. About 1870, the inn closed and was used as a private residence. A 1960s architectural study of the building showed it was extensively modified since its original construction. Today the building is used as law offices.

The Jonas Preston mansion was built in 1805 and has also been known as the Kirk house. It is located on Boot Road. This photograph was taken before the property was sold and carved up to make room for a car dealership in the 1970s. The Georgian mansion appears to have been built around a much earlier and smaller structure, as evidenced by the cooking fireplace and old stone walls in the basement. With extensive architectural details, it was one of the first post-Colonial homes built with material affluence in Newtown Square. It was owned for many years by the Kirk family who owned Kirk Chevrolet Agency just steps away. The original front of the home faces West Chester Pike, but today the main entrance is on Boot Road.

The William Lewis house on Goshen Road played a key role during the Revolutionary War. Built around 1708, the home served as an outpost for Maj. John Clarke, who was stationed here to watch troop movements along Goshen Road and report their movements to Gen. George Washington in Valley Forge. The farm complex remains next to this house as a separate property, and the original springhouse is located just on the other side of Goshen Road. The home's exterior remains largely unchanged in the last 50 years.

The Evan Lewis house, also known as the Echo Valley manor house and Harwick house, was built in 1719. This farmhouse-turned-mansion is located at 330 Echo Valley Road and is seen here in the 1970s. In 1818, the residence was considerably enlarged by Azariah Lewis. The home was owned for 150 years by the Lewis family; other owners included James Bartram and Harry Battles. Extensive repairs were done in 1904 to the stonework on the house, barn, and stone walls around the property, and it appears to remain in top condition today.

Very little is known about the Saw Mill Road house, which was once a tenant house for the large David Pratt house (around 1700 and 1852) across Saw Mill Road. Built in the 1700s, no nails were used in the original construction, and wooden pegs are visible in the attic. The home has one of the few remaining beehive ovens in the township. This photograph was taken in 2007 prior to the structure's complete restoration and expansion by a local builder. The Saw Mill Road house is a fine example of how historic homes can be saved, restored, and adopted for today's living needs.

The Jabez Lewis house was built around 1707. Shown in this 1970s photograph, it is located across from the Newtown Square Friends Meeting House along North Newtown Street Road. This home was used to hold meeting for Quakers in Newtown until the meetinghouse was built in 1711. In 1887, the property was sold. The house became part of the Pennsylvania Hospital Farm and was presumably used as a tenant house for farm workers. The hospital farm was sold in 1945, and the house became part of the St. Alban's residential tract. Containing two walk-in fireplaces, the home is being restored by its current owners, starting with the removal of the stucco exterior.

Often confused with an earlier photograph of the Square Tavern, this undated photograph of the Benjamin West house is the actual home that West lived in while his father was host of the Square Tavern at the opposite corner of Goshen and North Newtown Street Roads. The West family lived in this home between 1748 and 1755 (while Benjamin was between the ages of 10 and 17). The brick building is known to have been still standing in 1897 and was probably torn down in the early part of the 1900s. The modern photograph was taken from the steps of the Square Tavern.

The wheelwright shop, located at the beginning of the Route 252 bypass, was built around 1806. The building was originally operated as a blacksmith and wheelwright shop. At one time, it was converted into an art studio for artist Katherine Fussell. In 1979, it was converted to its current use as apartments.

The James Price house, built between 1700 and 1703, is located at the corner of Newtown and St. David's Roads. The smallest and oldest section of the house is at the rear of the main home. The larger section of the home was built in 1810. The barn was used for many years as a veterinary office for Dr. Raymond Giuliani.

Located down Paper Mill Road is another mill workers' house built in 1835. Like the Paper Mill House, this single-family home once consisted of three separate living quarters. This 1960s photograph shows the building before being expanded with a garage and a new metal roof. Today it is known as Paper Mill Farm.

The Iddings house, pictured here in the 1970s, is located off St. David's Road. Today it is part of the Harrison development and is being restored by its current owner. This two-and-a-half-story stucco-over-stone residence was built in two sections—the oldest part dates from the early 1700s, or possibly 1690, and has unusually thick fieldstone walls. There is a large cooking fireplace with a log beam mantel and old hardware. There have been significant additions over the years that have enlarged this estate. When the Harrison development was built, a second barn sat where the newer home for this property now exists.

The Iddings house was once the home of Gen. "Mad Anthony" Wayne's maternal grandparents, Richard and Margaret Iddings. It later became the home of the farm manager for the Harrison estate prior to being developed in the high-end Harrison residential development.

The Pratt homestead, pictured here in the 1920s, was one of many homes covered by the 391-acre Springton Reservoir. Despite the official name of Geist Reservoir, the Pratt family farm was named Springton, and the reservoir is widely known by this name.

Chapter 6

Institutional and Organizational Historic Sites

This photograph from about 1913 shows the Dunminning mansion, once a 15,000-square-foot estate located on St. David's Road bordering Radnor Township. The mansion was built in 1897 for John Brown, a wealthy Philadelphia banker, and built by architect T. P. Chandler, founder of the department of architecture at the University of Pennsylvania. Until recently, the mansion and surrounding 32 acres of grounds were used by the Devereux Foundation until it sold the property to Bentley Homes. After much protest by the historical society, the mansion was demolished in December 2007 to make way for an additional building lot in the high-end residential development on St. David's Road.

This 1929 photograph of the Women's Eastern Championship at Aronimink Golf Club appeared on the cover of the July issue of that year's *Golf Illustrated*. Located on St. David's Road, Aronimink Golf Club opened up its Donald Ross–designed course a year earlier, having moved from its previous location in Drexel Hill. Aronimink is consistently listed as one of the top 100 golf courses in the country. Built in 1928, the main clubhouse had extensive renovations completed in 2006. (Courtesy of Aronimink Golf Club/Golf Illustrated.)

Originally known as the Barrell and located on West Chester Pike, the original house was built in the mid-1800s. The Barrell name comes from the 1926 sesquicentennial in Philadelphia where the Hires Root Beer Company sold glasses of root beer from very large barrels (big enough to sit seven people). When the fair ended, a barrel was purchased and placed beside the house in Newtown Square. The building became a luncheon stand and later a tavern. At one time, the Barrell also sold gasoline. Since 1981 it has been operated as Charlotte's Restaurant.

This 2007 photograph shows the disrepair of this once-elegant mansion that was previously part of the north section of the DuPont estate. The Liseter Hall Farms mansion was also known as the Reece-Calvert house. Built in 1866, the building came into the possession of the Austin family, later the DuPont family by marriage. By the mid-1900s, the house was converted into two residences. One hundred and twenty-three acres of this section of the DuPont estate was sold to Episcopal Academy to create a new campus, which opened in the fall of 2008. The mansion, restored in 2008, includes an addition on the left/west side of the building and is now the development office for Episcopal Academy.

The Lewis springhouse, located on Goshen Road, was built around 1710 and restored by Vaughan and Sautter Builders when the springhouse development was built. The developer was recognized by the Delaware County Heritage Commission in 2006 for its restoration. Originally the Pennsylvania Department of Transportation had decreed that the springhouse be taken down for the entrance to Springhouse Lane; however, through patience and cooperation with the historical society and board of supervisors, the springhouse was saved by removing the original steps to the second floor along Goshen Road. It is currently maintained by the springhouse homeowner's association.

The Daniel Williamson house, located at 395 Bishop Hollow Road, is the oldest building in Newtown Township. Built in 1692 and now part of the Garrett-Williamson Foundation, the oldest section of the home is at the right end. Two additional sections were added on later with the middle section being vertical timber. Williamson was one of Newtown's earliest settlers. Stretton, England, where Williamson was born, is considered Newtown's sister town.

The Garrett-Williamson lodge, seen here in probably the 1960s, was built in 1916. Very little has changed on the exterior of the building since then. The lodge and what today is the Garrett-Williamson Foundation were rooted in the vision of Elizabeth Garrett's will when she passed away in 1910. Her will asked that the property be preserved as a farm and left for the enjoyment of those less fortunate. The lodge was used to hold classes when the Marple-Newtown High School burned down in 1956. The Ellis School also held classes there over the years.

The two gatehouses for the West Chester Pike entrance to Ellis College were located about where the new Medical Drive entrance to the Ellis Preserve is located. In 1920, two neighboring farms totaling 234 acres were purchased here, and construction began on Ellis College. The school, originally opened in 1918, was then located in Whitemarsh and officially opened at Newtown Square in 1923.

The Ellis College administrative building, also known as Ellis Hall and Main Hall, is seen here in the 1940s. It was built in 1932, designed by architect John Windrim. The Charles E. Ellis School for Girls was established in 1910 through the namesake's benefaction of $3.6 million. Ellis made his fortune in the early trolley systems of Philadelphia. Impressed with Stephen Girard and Girard College, Ellis wanted to do for girls what Girard did for orphaned boys. The building seen here shares many of the architectural characteristics of Founder's Hall at Girard College. The building had a major fire in 1950 and reopened in 1951.

This is a 1946 photograph of the Betsy Ross Cottage at Ellis College. The cottage was built in 1922 and designed by architect John Toorey along with three other original cottages. After years of financial trouble, the school finally closed in 1977. Today six of the cottages remain along with the administrative building, which will be incorporated into part of the Ellis Preserve/town center mixed-use development by BPG.

This elegant mansion was known as the Macafee House, Whitehouse, and Greenlands by Ellis College students. Ellis College sold the 313-acre campus to ARCO Chemical Company in 1978. In 1997, ARCO subdivided the land and sold 161 acres to SAP of North America. In June 2004, 149 acres were sold to BPG Development Company. It is not known when the mansion was demolished, but it was located approximately where the SAP America headquarters building is today.

The Newtown Square freight station was built in 1895 and is seen abandoned here in the 1980s at its original location where the Newtown Square branch of the Pennsylvania Railroad ended near Caley Road and North Newtown Street Road. In 1999, to make way for the Winding Way extension, the freight station was saved by being moved on a truck to its present location on West Chester Pike at the Drexel Lodge Park. This was paid for by the Newtown Square Historical Preservation Society, which began restoring the building. Shortly after, the Newtown Square Railroad Museum became a spin-off organization of the historical society and now maintains and restores old railroad cars. (Courtesy of Newtown Square Railroad Museum.)

In 1929, Drexel University (then Drexel Institute of Technology) purchased this 22-acre site and constructed the Drexel Lodge building in 1931. The property served as social recreation space for students from Drexel. The lodge contained dormitory-style rooms upstairs that could accommodate 50 people. The first floor had a large reception room with a fireplace, as well as a dance floor and stage. This May 1941 photograph is from a student-faculty day at the lodge.

This 2001 photograph shows a boarded-up Drexel Lodge looking east where the pavilion now stands at the township park. The township acquired the property, and after much controversy, the lodge was demolished around 2001. (Courtesy of Newtown Square Railroad Museum.)

This 35-room neoclassical-style mansion was built in 1916 by prominent architect Frank Miles Day for Charlton Yarnall, who owned Crum Creek Farm in Berwyn at the dawn of the 19th century. This property later became the Thoroughgood estate with reduced acreage, and it was converted into a nursing home. In June 1966, the Wayland Road mansion, with 20 acres of landscaped land and a swimming pool, was sold to Paul and Mildred Krental for $155,000 and converted into the Melmark Home for mentally and physically handicapped children. Although it has a Berwyn address, Melmark is actually located down White Horse Road in Newtown. The once-popular Delaware County Horse Show was held on the grounds of Melmark at one time. (Courtesy of Melmark Home.)